TOP TRUMPS
DINOSAURS

D0608735

© Haynes Publishing 2007

All rights reserved. No part of this publication may be reproduced or transmitted in any form or by any means, electronic or mechanical, including photocopying, recording or by any information storage or retrieval system, without permission in writing from Haynes Publishing.

This book is officially licensed by Winning Moves UK Ltd, owners of the Top Trumps registered trademark.

Tim Batty has asserted his right to be identified as the author of this book.

First published 2007. Reprinted 2008.

British Library Cataloguing-in-Publication Data:
A catalogue record for this book is available from the British Library

ISBN 978 1 84425 418 7

Library of Congress catalog card no. 2006936108

Published by Haynes Publishing,
Sparkford, Yeovil, Somerset BA22 7JJ, UK
Tel: +44 (0)1963 442030 Fax: +44 (0)1963 440001
Email: sales@haynes.co.uk
Website: www.haynes.co.uk

Haynes North America, Inc., 861 Lawrence Drive, Newbury Park California 91320, USA

Printed and bound in Great Britain by J. H. Haynes & Co. Ltd, Sparkford

Picture credits:
Front cover: *Tyrannosaurus rex charging* by John Sibbick
De Agostini/NHMPL: 14, 16-18, 28-29, 32-37, 42, 50-58, 64-65, 78, 88-90, 100-101, 104-109, 112-113, 116-118, 124-126, 130-133, 136-141, 144-145, 150, 160-162
Barislav Krzic/NHMPL: 24-25, 110
Gareth Monger: 46, 102, 128-129, 152-157, 168-170
Gareth Monger/NHMPL: 38, 146
Natural History Museum Picture Library (NHMPL): 80-82, 86, 142
John Sibbick: 20-22, 44-45, 84-85, 96-97, 114, 158
Chris Srnka: 8-13, 26, 30, 40-41, 48-49, 60-62, 66, 68-74, 92-94, 98, 120-122, 134, 148-149, 164-166, 172-186
Tim White/NHMPL: 76-77

The Author

Tim Batty was educated at the University of Wolverhampton before entering on a career in museums. He is a 'founding father' and curator of The Dinosaur Museum in Dorchester, and has been consultant on a number of books on dinosaurs.

TOP TRUMPS

DINOSAURS

Contents

About
Top Trumps

It's now more than 30 years since Britain's kids first caught the Top Trumps craze. The game remained hugely popular until the 1990s, when it slowly drifted into obscurity. Then, in 1999, UK games company Winning Moves discovered it, bought it, dusted it down, gave it a thorough makeover and introduced it to a whole new generation. And so the Top Trumps legend continues.

Nowadays, there are Top Trumps titles for just about everyone, with subjects about animals, cars, ships, aircraft and all the great films and TV shows. Top Trumps is now even more popular than before. In Britain, a pack of Top Trumps is bought every six seconds! And it's not just British children who love the game. Children in Australasia, the Far East, the Middle East, all over Europe and in North America can buy Top Trumps at their local shops.

Today you can even play the game on the internet, interactive DVD, your games console and even your mobile phone.

You've played the game...

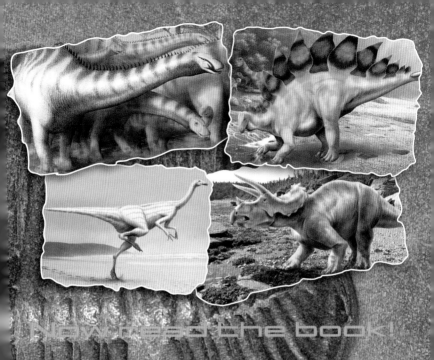

Now read the book!

Haynes Publishing and Top Trumps have teamed up to bring
you this exciting new Top Trumps book, in which you will find
even more pictures, details and statistics.

Top Trumps: Dinosaurs features 45 species of dinosaur,
from favourites such as Stegosaurus and Triceratops to
the unusual Therizinosaurus and, of course, the notorious
Tyrannosaurus rex. Packed with fascinating facts, stunning
pictures and all the vital statistics, this is the essential
pocket guide. And if you're lucky enough to spot any of these
dinosaurs, then at the back of the book we've provided space
for you to record when and where you saw them.

Look out for other Top Trumps books from Haynes Publishing
– even more facts, even more fun!

Allosaurus

Pronounced *Al-oh-saw-rus*

Allosaurus

Pronounced *Al-oh-saw-rus*

Allosaurus was one of the largest meat-eating dinosaurs of the late Jurassic and a top predator. Many fossils have been discovered in the USA where it would have preyed on the larger plant-eating dinosaurs. It was a fierce hunter using the long claws on its strong arms to grab prey, which was ripped to pieces by sharp, backward curving teeth contained in powerful jaws. Sauropods may also have formed part of the diet, especially if Allosaurus hunted in small packs of two or three. Apatosaurus bones have been found with teeth marks from an Allosaurus. Its legs were sturdy, with sharply clawed feet, but the speed at which it could run would have been limited by its size. Some skeletons have been found with bone injuries possibly caused by falling during the chase. The skull was about 80cm (2ft 7in) long and had a characteristic small bony ridge above each eye socket, measuring about 6cm (2.5in) high and 10cm (4in) long. Allosaurus' name 'different lizard' refers to the differently shaped vertebrae in its powerful neck.

Meaning	Different Lizard
When	Late Jurassic
Time	154–144 million years ago
Max length	12m (39ft)
Max height	4.6m (15ft)
Max weight	3,000kg (6,600lb)
Stance	Biped
Where	USA (Colorado, Utah, Wyoming) Portugal & Tanzania
Diet	Carnivore
Activity	Hunting, possibly in small packs
Intelligence	Medium
Named by	Othniel Charles Marsh
When named	1887
Order	Saurischia (Lizard-hipped)
Type	Theropoda, Tetanurae, Carnosauria

Late Cretaceous
99-65

Early Cretaceous
144-99

Late Jurassic
159-144

Middle Jurassic
190-159

Early Jurassic
205-190

Late Triassic
227-205

Middle Triassic
242-227

Early Triassic
245-242

Amargasaurus

Pronounced *Ah-mar-guh-saw-rus*

Amargasaurus

Pronounced *Ah-mar-guh-saw-rus*

The distinctive feature of Amargasaurus was a double row of spines attached to its neck, back and probably tail. The spines were tall at about 50cm (1ft 8in) high and more angled on the short neck, becoming shorter on the back and tail. The spines were extensions of the vertebrae in the backbone, and some of them were probably covered with a sail of skin either for use in heat regulation or for display purposes. Only one specimen has been discovered so far in the La Amarga region of Argentina after which it was named. The tail was missing from this specimen making an exact calculation of its length impossible. However it is thought that Amargasaurus was a medium sized sauropod similar in many ways to Diplodocus. Like all sauropods Amargasaurus had peg-like teeth for raking leaves off branches. However it could not chew so it needed to swallow gastroliths, which were stomach stones to help break up food in the stomach. These stones were rough when first swallowed but gradually got worn smooth.

Meaning	Amarga Lizard
When	Early Cretaceous
Time	132–127 million years ago
Max length	10m (39ft)
Max height	4m (13ft)
Max weight	10,000kg (22,000lb)
Stance	Quadruped
Where	Argentina
Diet	Herbivore
Activity	Grazing
Intelligence	Low
Named by	Leonardo Salgado & Jose Bonaparte
When named	1991
Order	Saurischia (Lizard-hipped)
Type	Sauropodomorpha, Sauropoda

Late Cretaceous
99-65

Early Cretaceous
144-99

Late Jurassic
159-144

Middle Jurassic
190-159

Early Jurassic
205-190

Late Triassic
227-205

Middle Triassic
242-227

Early Triassic
245-242

Ankylosaurus

Pronounced *An-key-low-saw-rus*

Ankylosaurus

Pronounced *An-key-low-saw-rus*

Ankylosaurus was an extremely well-armoured dinosaur. Its back and sides were covered with rows of bony spikes, nodules and plates embedded in the skin. The tail ended in a large bony club, weighing at least 50kg, a distinguishing characteristic between ankylosaurids and nodosaurids. The tail club was an excellent weapon, which could be swung on the end of the tail to deter any predators. The head was protected by two spikes jutting out from each side. The underbelly was the only vulnerable part of the body. It could be protected if Ankylosaurus crouched down and presented attackers with a body completely covered with bony spikes and plates. Ankylosaurus' size and weight made it slow moving. Its mouth had a horny toothless beak for attacking plants, and leaf-shaped cheek teeth for chewing and grinding up food prior to swallowing. It was one of the last of the ankylosaurids living at the end of the dinosaur era, just before the mass extinction that killed all dinosaurs, and many other creatures.

Statistics

Meaning	Fused Lizard
When	Late Cretaceous
Time	71–65 million years ago
Max length	10.6m (34ft 6ins)
Max height	3m (9ft 9ins)
Max weight	4,500kg (9,900lb)
Stance	Quadruped
Where	USA (Wyoming, Montana), Canada (Alberta)
Diet	Herbivore
Activity	Grazing
Intelligence	Low
Named by	Barnum Brown
When named	1908
Order	Ornithischia (Bird-hipped)
Type	Thyreophora, Ankylosauria

Timeline
Million Years Ago

Late Cretaceous 99–65

Early Cretaceous 144–99

Late Jurassic 159–144

Middle Jurassic 190–159

Early Jurassic 205–190

Late Triassic 227–205

Middle Triassic 242–227

Early Triassic 245–242

Archaeopteryx

Pronounced *Ark-ee-op-tur-iks*

Archaeopteryx

Pronounced *Ark-ee-op-tur-iks*

Archaeopteryx is the original 'missing link' between dinosaurs and birds. It has some characteristics of birds such as feathers, a wishbone and wings, whilst still exhibiting some dinosaurian qualities – teeth, three-clawed hands, and a bony tail. All the specimens of Archaeopteryx have been found in the Solenhofen limestone of Bavaria, Germany. This limestone is extremely smooth and fine-grained making it possible for very detailed fossils to be preserved. Archaeopteryx had four claws on its feet, three facing forwards and one backwards. The feathers are designed for flight but Archaeopteryx could only fly for very short periods of time. The muscles used when flapping the wings were anchored onto the breastbone, which was small, and indicates that the flight muscles were weak. There are two views on how flight was achieved. One is that by using its claws Archaeopteryx would climb into a tree and launch itself into the air. The other view is that it would have achieved flight by running along the ground, jumping and flapping its wings.

Statistics

Meaning	Ancient Feather
When	Late Jurassic
Time	150–144 million years ago
Max length	0.6m (2ft)
Max height	0.2m (8in)
Max weight	0.5kg (1lb 2oz)
Stance	Biped
Where	Germany
Diet	Carnivore
Activity	Hunting
Intelligence	High
Named by	Hermann von Meyer
When named	1861
Order	Saurischia (Lizard-hipped)
Type	Theropoda, Tetanurae, Coelurosauria

Timeline
Million Years Ago

Late Cretaceous
99–65

Early Cretaceous
144–99

Late Jurassic
159–144

Middle Jurassic
190–159

Early Jurassic
205–190

Late Triassic
227–205

Middle Triassic
242–227

Early Triassic
245–242

Baryonyx

Pronounced *Ba-ree-on-ix*

Baryonyx

Pronounced *Ba-ree-on-ix*

Baryonx is different from most other theropods in several ways. The elongated skull is much like that of a crocodile in shape and the neck is straight. The jaws contain 96 small, serrated teeth, more than is usual in theropods. The gigantic 25cm (10in) claw-bone on the three-fingered hand distinguishes Baryonyx from other dinosaurs. Baryonyx was mainly a two-legged animal, but possibly walked on all fours for some of the time. The jaws and teeth, and the finding of fish scales from the fish Lepidotes in the rib cage, suggest that Baryonx ate fish rather than meat. However it may well have scavenged meat as well. Iguanodon bones were found with the Baryonyx remains. It lived on land, along the banks of the rivers or swamps probably hunting in a similar style to bears today. William Walker, an amateur fossil hunter, discovered the large claw-bone in 1983 at a clay-pit, near Dorking in Surrey, England. The new dinosaur was named Baryonx walkeri after its distinguishing feature and the person who found it.

Statistics

Meaning	Heavy Claw
When	Early Cretaceous
Time	127–121 million years ago
Max length	10m (32ft 6in)
Max height	4.5m (14ft 7in)
Max weight	2,000kg (4,400lb)
Stance	Biped
Where	England
Diet	Carnivore
Activity	Hunting along river banks
Intelligence	Medium
Named by	Alan Charig & Angela Milner
When named	1986
Order	Saurischia (Lizard-hipped)
Type	Theropoda, Tetanurae

Timeline
Million Years Ago

Late Cretaceous
99-65

Early Cretaceous
144-99

Late Jurassic
159-144

Middle Jurassic
190-159

Early Jurassic
205-190

Late Triassic
227-205

Middle Triassic
242-227

Early Triassic
245-242

Brachiosaurus

Pronounced *Brack-ee-oh-saw-rus*

Brachiosaurus

Pronounced *Brack-ee-oh-saw-rus*

This massive dinosaur is one of the largest animals to have ever walked on land. It is 13 times heavier than an adult male African elephant and over twice as tall as a male giraffe – the tallest living animal today. The front legs were much longer than the rear ones causing the back to slope upwards towards the head. The humerus (upper bone in front legs) was over 2 metres (6ft 6in) long, and combined with a long neck gave Brachiosaurus its great height. This was an advantage as it could feed off the tallest trees out of reach of smaller sauropods. It had peg-like teeth, which were excellent for stripping leaves off branches. These were ground up and digested in the stomach by gastroliths (stomach stones) and microbes. Brachiosaurus had a small head with a crest and nostrils facing upwards. This led to the mistaken idea that Brachiosaurus may have partly lived in deep lakes, using its long neck as a type of snorkel. Brachiosaurus is the largest dinosaur with a complete skeleton on display, in the Natural History Museum in Berlin.

Meaning	Arm Lizard
When	Late Jurassic
Time	154–144 million years ago
Max length	26m (84ft 6in)
Max height	13m (42ft 3in)
Max weight	70,000kg (154,300lb)
Stance	Quadruped
Where	USA (Colorado, Utah), Tanzania
Diet	Herbivore
Activity	Grazing on tall trees
Intelligence	Low
Named by	Elmer Riggs
When named	1903
Order	Saurischia (Lizard-hipped)
Type	Sauropodomorpha, Sauropoda

Late Cretaceous
99–65

Early Cretaceous
144–99

Late Jurassic
159–144

Middle Jurassic
190–159

Early Jurassic
205–190

Late Triassic
227–205

Middle Triassic
242–227

Early Triassic
245–242

Camarasaurus

Pronounced *Cam-a-rah-saw-rus*

Camarasaurus

Pronounced *Cam-a-rah-saw-rus*

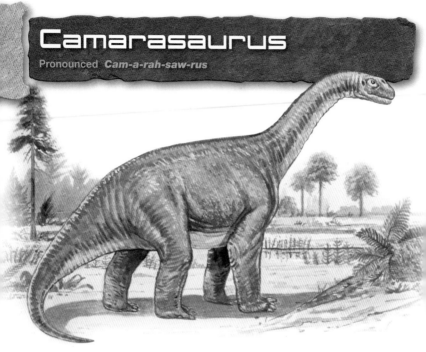

Camarasaurus, like all sauropods, had four sturdy elephant-like legs supporting its large body. Hollow spaces, or chambers, in the backbone helped to reduce the weight of the neck and gave this dinosaur its name. The head was short and lofty with a mouth full of spoon-shaped teeth about 11cm (4.5in) long. These were stronger than those of other sauropods indicating that it fed off tough vegetation. Many specimens of Camarasaurus have been found in the Morrison Formation, a band of rock centred on Wyoming and Colorado, which is rich in dinosaur finds. In 1877 it became the site for the famous 'bone wars' been two early collectors Edward Drinker Cope (who named Camarasaurus) and Othniel Charles Marsh. There was intense rivalry between the two and gunfights were even had over some dinosaur discoveries! Young and adult skeletons of Camarasaurus have been found together in large groups showing that it lived and travelled in herds, probably searching for food, and indicating the adults cared for the young in some way.

Statistics

Meaning	Chambered Lizard
When	Late Jurassic
Time	154–144 million years ago
Max length	18m (58ft 6in)
Max height	4.6m (15ft) at hips
Max weight	20,000kg (44,100lb)
Stance	Quadruped
Where	USA (Wyoming, Colorado, Utah, New Mexico)
Diet	Herbivore
Activity	Grazing
Intelligence	Low
Named by	Edward Drinker Cope
When named	1877
Order	Saurischia (Lizard-hipped)
Type	Sauropodomorpha, Sauropoda

Timeline
Million Years Ago

Late Cretaceous
99–65

Early Cretaceous
144–99

Late Jurassic
159–144

Middle Jurassic
190–159

Early Jurassic
205–190

Late Triassic
227–205

Middle Triassic
242–227

Early Triassic
245–242

Carcharodontosaurus

Carcharodontosaurus

Pronounced *Car-sha-oh-dont-oh-saw-rus*

Named after the great white shark, Carcharodontosaurus' teeth were triangular and serrated along both the front and back edges, and up to 20 centimetres (8 in) long. The tooth shape suggests that this dinosaur may have eaten fish as part of its diet, although it is more probable that it hunted large plant-eating dinosaurs including sauropods. The first remains of Carcharodontosaurus, discovered in the 1920s in Egypt, were housed in the Bavarian Museum in Munich, Germany and destroyed by Allied bombing in 1944 during World War 2. It was not until 1996 that Paul Sereno discovered the remains of a second Carcharodontosaurus in Morocco. He found a skull and a few associated bones. The skull proved to be larger than T rex's at 1.6 metres (5ft 2in). A close relative of Carcharodontosaurus is the massive Giganotosaurus, which is known from South America. Africa and South America were joined forming part of Gondwana, a super-continent, right up until the beginning of the Cretaceous period and so these two dinosaurs could have shared a common ancestor.

Statistics

Meaning	Shark-toothed Lizard
When	Cretaceous
Time	112–94 million years ago
Max length	14m (45ft 6in)
Max height	4m (13ft)
Max weight	7,200kg (15,800lb)
Stance	Biped
Where	Egypt, Morocco, Tunisia, Algeria, Libya & Niger
Diet	Carnivore
Activity	Hunting
Intelligence	Medium
Named by	Ernst Stromer
When named	1931
Order	Saurischia (Lizard-hipped)
Type	Theropoda, Tetanurae, Carnosauria

Timeline
Million Years Ago

Late Cretaceous
99-65

Early Cretaceous
144-99

Late Jurassic
159-144

Middle Jurassic
190-159

Early Jurassic
205-190

Late Triassic
227-205

Middle Triassic
242-227

Early Triassic
245-242

Carnotaurus

Pronounced *Car-no-taw-rus*

Carnotaurus

Pronounced *Car-no-taw-rus*

Carnotaurus is only known from one almost complete skeleton found in Patagonia, Argentina. It was a strange looking theropod with a large head but short snout giving the face of a dinosaur 'bulldog'. This feature and the two heavy horns over the eyes give Carnotaurus its name. Despite this large strong head and neck, the lower jaw was light and weak, showing that it might have scavenged for food. The horns were most likely used by males when competing for mates, just like deer do today. Carnotaurus had very short weak arms, the purpose of which is not known. The two lower arm bones were incredibly short, ending in a hand with four small fingers, one of which was a spike. Along with the skeleton a large skin impression of the right side of the dinosaur was recovered. This showed that Carnotaurus had a scaly reptilian type of skin composed of large, round scales arranged in rows over the body.

Statistics

Meaning	Meat-eating Bull
When	Late Cretaceous
Time	84–65 million years ago
Max length	7.5m (24ft 4in)
Max height	4m (13ft)
Max weight	1,000kg (2,200lb)
Stance	Biped
Where	Argentina
Diet	Carnivore
Activity	Scavenging or hunting
Intelligence	Medium
Named by	Jose Bonaparte
When named	1985
Order	Saurischia (Lizard-hipped)
Type	Theropoda, Ceratosauria

Timeline
Million Years Ago

Late Cretaceous
99–65

Early Cretaceous
144–99

Late Jurassic
159–144

Middle Jurassic
190–159

Early Jurassic
205–190

Late Triassic
227–205

Middle Triassic
242–227

Early Triassic
245–242

Ceratosaurus

Pronounced *See-rat-oh-saw-rus*

Ceratosaurus

Pronounced *See-rat-oh-saw-rus*

Ceratosaurus had two brow horns or ridges above the eyes and a large horn on the snout, from which its name is taken. The horns were probably used for display purposes when competing for a mate. Unusually for a theropod it had a jagged crest of small bony plates running the length of its neck, back and tail. Their purpose is not known. Both Allosaurus and Ceratosaurus remains have been found in the Dinosaur National Monument in the USA, and in Tendaguru in Tanzania, making them rivals for the same food sources. Allosaurus was the larger and more developed and would have had the advantage. Ceratosaurus was a primitive theropod and exhibited two unusual features: it had four sharply clawed fingers on each hand instead of the usual three, and the tail was flexible. More advanced theropods had tails that were stiffened by tendons to give balance, and because of this are classified as tetanurans. It is likely that Ceratosaurus hunted in small packs preying on small or young dinosaurs.

Statistics

Meaning	Horned Lizard
When	Late Jurassic
Time	154–144 million years ago
Max length	6m (19ft 6in)
Max height	3m (9ft 9in)
Max weight	1,300kg (2,900lb)
Stance	Biped
Where	USA (Colorado, Utah), Tanzania
Diet	Carnivore
Activity	Hunting
Intelligence	Medium
Named by	Othniel Charles Marsh
When named	1884
Order	Saurischia (Lizard-hipped)
Type	Theropoda, Ceratosauria

Timeline
Million Years Ago

Late Cretaceous
99–65

Early Cretaceous
144–99

Late Jurassic
159–144

Middle Jurassic
190–159

Early Jurassic
205–190

Late Triassic
227–205

Middle Triassic
242–227

Early Triassic
245–242

Coelophysis

Pronounced *See-low-fy-sis*

TOP TRUMPS

Coelophysis

Pronounced *See-low-fy-sis*

Many fossil skeletons of Coelophysis have been found together in what are known as 'bone beds'. Ghost Ranch in New Mexico is one such site. These mass deaths, which contained both adult and young, demonstrate that Coelophysis lived in groups. The large number of skeletons was most likely caused by a disaster such as a sudden flood. Two types of Coelophysis are known, one larger and heavier than the other, probably showing the difference between male and female. It was thought that this dinosaur was cannibalistic as some skeletons were found with what appeared to be the bones of young Coelophysis inside what would have been the stomach. However recent research has suggested these bones could belong to crocodiles. This still does not answer the problem of how baby Coelophysis bones have been found in its coprolites – fossilised dinosaur droppings. Coelophysis was lightly built making it an agile and speedy hunter of lizards and other small reptiles. It lived in packs, which offered protection against larger predators, and relative safety for the young.

Statistics

Meaning	Hollow Form
When	Late Triassic
Time	227–210 million years ago
Max length	2.8m (9ft 2in)
Max height	1m (3ft 3in)
Max weight	45kg (99lbs)
Stance	Biped
Where	USA (New Mexico, Arizona, Utah)
Diet	Carnivore
Activity	Hunting
Intelligence	High
Named by	Edward Drinker Cope
When named	1889
Order	Saurischia (Lizard-hipped)
Type	Theropoda

Timeline
Million Years Ago

Late Cretaceous
99-65

Early Cretaceous
144-99

Late Jurassic
159-144

Middle Jurassic
190-159

Early Jurassic
205-190

Late Triassic
227-205

Middle Triassic
242-227

Early Triassic
245-242

Compsognathus

Pronounced *Comp-sog-nay-thus*

Compsognathus

Pronounced *Comp-sog-nay-thus*

Compsognathus was only the size of a chicken but with a long tail and long legs. It is one of the smallest dinosaurs known. Its bones were hollow, typical for a coelurosaur, making it lightweight and very fast. Only two skeletons have been found, one in Germany and one in France. The German skeleton was complete and found in the fine-grained Solnhofen Limestone of Bavaria, close in geological time and place to Archaeopteryx. At the end of the Jurassic what is now Germany was covered with shallow lagoons and islands. The soft mud of the lagoons allowed many delicate creatures to be fossilised, protecting them from scavengers or fast currents. Archaeopteryx probably evolved from Compsognathus or a similar type of dinosaur. Fossilised unhatched eggs were found with this specimen. Compsognathus had bird-like feet with three clawed toes, and a very small fourth toe pointing backwards. The hands had two fingers with small claws. It would have lived on the land adjacent to the lagoons hunting small reptiles – a lizard has been found in one of the skeletons.

Meaning	Pretty Jaw
When	Late Jurassic
Time	151–144 million years ago
Max length	0.6m (2ft)
Max height	0.3m (1ft)
Max weight	3kg (6.5lb)
Stance	Biped
Where	Germany & France
Diet	Carnivore (small reptiles)
Activity	Hunting
Intelligence	High
Named by	Johann Wagner
When named	1859
Order	Saurischia (Lizard-hipped)
Type	Theropoda, Tetanurae, Coelurosauria

Timeline
Million Years Ago

Period	Million Years Ago
Late Cretaceous	99–65
Early Cretaceous	144–99
Late Jurassic	159–144
Middle Jurassic	190–159
Early Jurassic	205–190
Late Triassic	227–205
Middle Triassic	242–227
Early Triassic	245–242

Dilophosaurus

Pronounced *Die-loaf-oh-saw-rus*

Dilophosaurus

Pronounced *Die-loaf-oh-saw-rus*

This strange-looking dinosaur takes its name from the pair of large curved bony crests on each side of the head. After the first discovery of three skeletons in 1942 it was wrongly identified as a new species of Megalosaurus, because the skulls were poorly preserved. In 1964 Samuel Welles returned to the site and discovered a fourth specimen which clearly showed the two crests. The dinosaur was renamed Dilophosaurus in 1970. The crests were fragile and most probably just for display purposes. Not all the skeletons have been found with crests so they could be an indicator of the males. The head is large with strong jaws and sharp teeth. Dilophosaurus would have had to have captured, killed and torn up its prey with its claws. Otherwise it would need to scavenge food, as its teeth were too weak to kill a struggling dinosaur. Like Ceratosaurus the hands had four fingers, three of which were useable, the fourth was very small. Dilophosaurus most likely hunted in packs, when not scavenging off carcasses of dead dinosaurs.

Statistics

Meaning	Two-ridged Lizard
When	Early Jurassic
Time	202–190 million years ago
Max length	6m (19ft 6in)
Max height	2.5m (8ft 2in)
Max weight	500kg (1,100lb)
Stance	Biped
Where	USA (Arizona), China
Diet	Carnivore
Activity	Hunting and scavenging
Intelligence	Medium
Named by	Samuel Welles
When named	1954
Order	Saurischia (Lizard-hipped)
Type	Theropoda, Ceratosauria

Timeline
Million Years Ago

Late Cretaceous
99-65

Early Cretaceous
144-99

Late Jurassic
159-144

Middle Jurassic
190-159

Early Jurassic
205-190

Late Triassic
227-205

Middle Triassic
242-227

Early Triassic
245-242

Diplodocus

Pronounced *Dee-plod-oh-cus*

Diplodocus

Pronounced *Dee-plod-oh-cus*

For a long time Diplodocus was known as the longest dinosaur. However, Seismosaurus stole this record when it was discovered, at an amazing 40m long. Over half of Diplodocus' length was made up of its tail at 14m (45ft 6in) long. Its strange name is taken from the curious shape of the tailbones, which have projections underneath, front and back, to give protection to the blood vessels flowing along the tail. Its head, neck and tail were carried parallel to the ground at back height. The skull was small for such a large animal, only 60cm (2ft) long, and had peg-like teeth for raking leaves from conifer trees. Diplodocus' large size deterred many potential attackers, but against larger carnosaurs, such as Allosaurus, it could swing its tail whip-like to ward of an attack. Strong tendons along the spine made the tail a very effective weapon. Footprints and accumulations of skeletons show that Diplodocus moved slowly and lived in herds, probably feeding off the vegetation in one area before migrating to a new area once that vegetation was used up.

Statistics

Meaning	Double-Beam
When	Late Jurassic
Time	154–144 million years ago
Max length	27m (87ft 9in)
Max height	4m (13ft) at hips
Max weight	12,000kg (26,455lb)
Stance	Quadruped
Where	USA (Colorado, Montana, Utah, Wyoming)
Diet	Herbivore
Activity	Grazing
Intelligence	Low
Named by	Othniel Charles Marsh
When named	1878
Order	Saurischia (Lizard-hipped)
Type	Sauropodomorpha, Sauropoda

Timeline
Million Years Ago

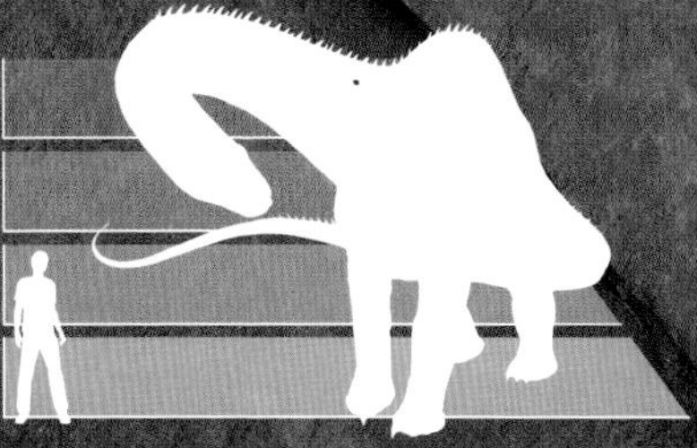

Late Cretaceous
99-65

Early Cretaceous
144-99

Late Jurassic
159-144

Middle Jurassic
190-159

Early Jurassic
205-190

Late Triassic
227-205

Middle Triassic
242-227

Early Triassic
245-242

Eoraptor

Pronounced *Ee-oh-rap-tor*

Eoraptor was small about the size of a dog, and was one of the earliest dinosaurs. It was a very primitive theropod with five fingered hands, two of which, the fourth and fifth, were shortened. The head was slim with a variety of teeth. The upper jaw had sharp, slightly serrated teeth as is normal in a theropod, whilst the lower jaw had leaf-shaped teeth similar to those of prosauropods. It hunted small reptiles and lizards, catching them in its grasping hands before eating them. Eoraptor was discovered in the Valley of the Moon in the Ishigualasto Basin of northwest Argentina. The area has a moon-like appearance today, but in Triassic times it was a river valley with trees and vegetation. It formed part of Gondwana, a super-continent of what are now South America, Africa, Australia, Antarctica and India. These continental plates gradually split and moved to where they are today through a process of continental drift. Remains of Herrerasaurus and Pisanosaurus, an early ornithischian, have also been found at this site.

Statistics

Meaning	Dawn Thief
When	Late Triassic
Time	227–221 million years ago
Max length	1m (3ft 3ins)
Max height	0.5m (1ft 7in)
Max weight	10kg (22lb)
Stance	Biped
Where	Argentina
Diet	Carnivore
Activity	Hunting
Intelligence	High
Named by	Paul Sereno, C. Forster, R. Rogers & A. Monetta
When named	1993
Order	Saurischia (Lizard-hipped)
Type	Theropoda

Timeline
Million Years Ago

Late Cretaceous
99-65

Early Cretaceous
144-99

Late Jurassic
159-144

Middle Jurassic
190-159

Early Jurassic
205-190

Late Triassic
227-205

Middle Triassic
242-227

Early Triassic
245-242

Gallimimus

Pronounced *Gal-ee-me-mus*

Gallimimus

Pronounced *Gal-ee-me-mus*

Gallimimus was the largest of the ornithomimid, or ostrich dinosaurs. It differed from its American cousins, such as Ornithomimus and Struthiomimus, chiefly in the shape of the skull. The head was long and thin, with a toothless beak similar to a bird. The eyes were large and facing sideways preventing binocular vision. The body was relatively small with a long neck, which held the head above the body in the classic ostrich style, and the tail was long. Gallimimus was most probably covered with downy feathers, not suitable for flight, but good for insulation. This implies that it was a warm-blooded dinosaur. The long legs had hollow bones making them lightweight but strong and affording Gallimimus the ability to run speedily – probably as fast as a modern ostrich. Gallimimus was mainly a carnivore with a diet of small reptiles and mammals and probably insects. However, it may also have eaten eggs and possibly plants. Its hands were certainly suitable for digging eggs from nests. The only means of defence against large meat-eating dinosaurs was its speed, and it was one of the fastest dinosaurs.

Statistics

Meaning	Chicken Mimic
When	Late Cretaceous
Time	71–65 million years ago
Max length	6m (19ft 6in)
Max height	2.3m (7ft 5in)
Max weight	450kg (990lb)
Stance	Biped
Where	Mongolia
Diet	Omnivore
Activity	Hunting or grazing
Intelligence	High
Named by	Halszka Osmólska, Roniewicz & Barsbold
When named	1972
Order	Saurischia (Lizard-hipped)
Type	Theropoda, Tetanurae, Coelurosauria

Timeline
Million Years Ago

Late Cretaceous
99–65

Early Cretaceous
144–99

Late Jurassic
159–144

Middle Jurassic
190–159

Early Jurassic
205–190

Late Triassic
227–205

Middle Triassic
242–227

Early Triassic
245–242

Giganotosaurus

Pronounced *Jig-an-oh-saw-rus*

Giganotosaurus

Pronounced *Jig-an-oh-saw-rus*

In 1993 when Giganotosaurus was discovered it took the record from Tyrannosaurus rex for being the largest meat-eating dinosaur. It was a massive beast with a skull that was 1.8 metres (6ft) long, as long as a man is tall. However its brain was smaller than T rex's. The jaws were full of teeth up to 20 centimetres (8in) long that were designed for slicing through flesh, rather than crunching bones as in the case of T rex. It was a powerful dinosaur, with arms that were short and strong with three-fingered hands and claws. Typically, as with most large carnosaurs, the legs were sturdy and not built for running fast, and the feet had three main toes with a much-shortened fourth toe. Giganotosaurus most likely preyed on the large sauropods that lived at the same time. A skeleton of one was found near the remains of Giganotosaurus. It would have needed to hunt in small packs to kill an adult sauropod, but on its own Giganotosaurus could kill an injured or young sauropod.

Meaning	Giant Southern Lizard
When	Early Cretaceous
Time	112–99 million years ago
Max length	13.7m (44ft 6in)
Max height	5m (16ft 3in)
Max weight	8,000kg (17,600lb)
Stance	Biped
Where	Argentina
Diet	Carnivore
Activity	Hunting
Intelligence	Medium
Named by	Rodolfo Coria & Leonardo Salgado
When named	1995
Order	Saurischia (Lizard-hipped)
Type	Theropoda, Tetanurae, Carnosauria

Late Cretaceous
99–65

Early Cretaceous
144–99

Late Jurassic
159–144

Middle Jurassic
190–159

Early Jurassic
205–190

Late Triassic
227–205

Middle Triassic
242–227

Early Triassic
245–242

Herrerasaurus

Pronounced *Her-ray-rah-saw-rus*

Herrarasaurus and Eoraptor were both very early theropod dinosaurs that lived in what is now the Ishigualasto Basin of northwestern Argentina. Herrarasaurus was the larger of the two, the more developed and the dominant. It had three long clawed fingers on each hand, and two further shortened stumpy fingers. The head was long and narrow, with curved pointed teeth. A flexible joint in the lower jaw gave a much more effective bite. During the Late Triassic there were few predators and this dinosaur with its powerful legs, long flexible tail and larger build would have had the advantage in speed and agility. It probably preyed on rhynchosaurs, squat pig-like plant-eating animals such as Scaphonyx, small reptiles and even Pisanosaurus, an early plant-eating dinosaur. Fossil records indicate that the area had a wet and a dry season at that time. It would also have scavenged off carcasses when the opportunity arose. Herrerasaurus takes its name from Victorino Herrera, a farmer, who discovered the first skeleton in 1963.

Statistics

Meaning	Herrera's Lizard
When	Late Triassic
Time	227–221 million years ago
Max length	3m (9ft 9in)
Max height	1.5m (4ft 10in)
Max weight	220kg (485lb)
Stance	Biped
Where	Argentina
Diet	Carnivore
Activity	Hunting
Intelligence	High
Named by	Paul Sereno
When named	1988
Order	Saurischia (Lizard-hipped)
Type	Theropoda

Timeline
Million Years Ago

Late Cretaceous
99-65

Early Cretaceous
144-99

Late Jurassic
159-144

Middle Jurassic
190-159

Early Jurassic
205-190

Late Triassic
227-205

Middle Triassic
242-227

Early Triassic
245-242

Hypsilophodon
Pronounced *Hip-see-loff-oh-don*

Hypsilophodon

Pronounced *Hip-see-loff-oh-don*

Hypsilophodon remains have been misunderstood over the years. Originally when it was first discovered in 1849 it was thought to be a young Iguanodon, until Thomas Huxley finally recognised it as a new species of dinosaur. It was also thought to live in the trees like the modern tree kangaroo, and shown in that way. Hypsilophodon was actually a swift-running dinosaur that grazed the low vegetation, such as horsetails and ferns. It was well adapted for foraging with a strong beak for nipping off leaves and fronds, and strong, ridged teeth for chewing the vegetation. It had developed cheek pouches, which aided chewing and meant food could be stored. Groups of skeletons have been found together indicating that this animal lived in herds. The Isle of Wight has yielded many fossil finds of this dinosaur. Its only means of defence was to flee from its attackers. It was an early ornithopod, still having five fingers and four toes instead of the four fingers and three toes of the more highly developed ornithopods.

Meaning	High-ridged Tooth
When	Early Cretaceous
Time	127–112 million years ago
Max length	2.3m (7ft 6in)
Max height	0.9m (2ft 11in)
Max weight	30kg (66lb)
Stance	Biped
Where	England, Spain, & USA (South Dakota)
Diet	Herbivore
Activity	Grazing
Intelligence	Medium
Named by	Thomas Huxley
When named	1869
Order	Ornithischia (Bird-hipped)
Type	Ornithopoda

Late Cretaceous
99-65

Early Cretaceous
144-99

Late Jurassic
159-144

Middle Jurassic
190-159

Early Jurassic
205-190

Late Triassic
227-205

Middle Triassic
242-227

Early Triassic
245-242

Iguanodon

Pronounced *Ig-wah-no-don*

Iguanodon

Pronounced *Ig-wah-no-don*

This was the second dinosaur to be scientifically named. Gideon Mantell's wife Mary made the original discovery of a tooth in Sussex, England. Further teeth and bones followed and the similarity between the teeth and a modern iguana lizard's teeth was noticed. Life-size statues of both Iguanodon and Megalosaurus were produced in the 1850s for the grounds of the Crystal Palace in London, where they still stand today. These early reconstructions were wrong in many ways but were important first steps in interpreting how dinosaurs looked. Famously the thumb-spike of Iguanodon was placed on the nose as a horn. During the 1880s over 30 skeletons of Iguanodon were discovered in a coalmine in Bernissart, Belgium. Iguanodon is now seen as mainly a four-legged dinosaur; the front legs are shorter than the thick hind ones and three of the fingers form a pad. It may have reared up on its hind legs to feed. Behind a horny beak, Iguanodon had numerous teeth in both jaws, with which it could grind up vegetation.

Statistics

Meaning	Iguana Tooth
When	Early Cretaceous
Time	137–121 million years ago
Max length	9m (30ft)
Max height	5m (16ft 3in)
Max weight	4,500kg (9,900lb)
Stance	Mainly Quadruped
Where	England, Belgium, Mongolia, & USA (Utah)
Diet	Herbivore
Activity	Grazing, probably in herds
Intelligence	Medium
Named by	Gideon Mantell
When named	1825
Order	Ornithiscia (Bird-hipped)
Type	Ornithopoda

Timeline
Million Years Ago

Late Cretaceous
99–65

Early Cretaceous
144–99

Late Jurassic
159–144

Middle Jurassic
190–159

Early Jurassic
205–190

Late Triassic
227–205

Middle Triassic
242–227

Early Triassic
245–242

Kentrosaurus

Pronounced *Kent-row-saw-rus*

TOP TRUMPS 89

Kentrosaurus

Pronounced *Kent-row-saw-rus*

Kentrosaurus is the African cousin of the larger Stegosaurus, which is only found in North America. It was an armoured dinosaur with a double row of smaller plates over its back from its head. These then became a double row of spikes, up to 60 centimetres (2ft) long, from above the hind legs and all along the tail. The spikes and plates were paired rather than staggered as was the case with Stegosaurus. There was an extra spike jutting out from the side of the dinosaur. This was originally placed on the hip but is now thought to belong on the shoulder. Its front legs were much shorter than the rear ones meaning that its head was close to the ground. It fed on low growing plants such as ferns. It could only move slowly and most likely lived in herds. Its chief predators were the large carnosaurs of the time. Hundreds of bones of Kentrosaurus were discovered in 1909 in the Tendaguru Hills of Tanzania, a site rich in fossil finds.

Statistics

Meaning	Spiky Lizard
When	Late Jurassic
Time	154–151 million years ago
Max length	5m (16ft 3in)
Max height	2.5m (8ft 2in)
Max weight	1,800kg (3,900lb)
Stance	Quadruped
Where	Tanzania
Diet	Herbivore
Activity	Grazing
Intelligence	Low
Named by	Edwin Henning
When named	1915
Order	Ornithischia (Bird-hipped)
Type	Thyreophora, Stegosauria

Timeline
Million Years Ago

Late Cretaceous
99–65

Early Cretaceous
144–99

Late Jurassic
159–144

Middle Jurassic
190–159

Early Jurassic
205–190

Late Triassic
227–205

Middle Triassic
242–227

Early Triassic
245–242

Lambeosaurus

Pronounced *Lamb-ee-oh-saw-rus*

Lambeosaurus

Pronounced *Lamb-ee-oh-saw-rus*

Discovered in 1889 by Lawrence Lambe, after whom it was named, Lambeosaurus was the largest of the duck-billed dinosaurs. Duck-billed dinosaurs are so called because of the shape of their mouth, which is broad and flattened, similar to the mouth of a duck. Lambeosaurus' head crest was rectangular in shape and filled with hollow nasal passages. The crests were most likely used for display purposes, and to amplify calls to warn of danger, or to attract mates. They would also have served to aid recognition of different types of duck-billed dinosaurs. Behind the crest was a backward pointing spike, which was composed of solid bone. Lambeosaurus lived in herds, probably mixed with other types of duck-billed dinosaurs and grazed off low growing plants. Duck-billed dinosaurs were abundant and the equivalent of the cow today. Fossilised skin impressions have been found showing that it was scaly in texture. Hand impressions have been discovered showing that a web-like covering of skin joined the fingers. This was originally thought to show that Lambeosaurus lived in the water, but this idea has since been dropped.

Meaning	Lambe's Lizard
When	Late Cretaceous
Time	84–71 million years ago
Max length	15m (48ft 9in)
Max height	4m (13ft)
Max weight	4,500kg (9,900lb)
Stance	Quadruped
Where	USA (Montana, Wyoming, Utah, Colorado, New Mexico) Canada (Alberta)
Diet	Herbivore
Activity	Grazing
Intelligence	Medium
Named by	William Parks
When named	1923
Order	Ornithischia (Bird-hipped)
Type	Ornithopoda, Hadrosauria

Late Cretaceous
99-65

Early Cretaceous
144-99

Late Jurassic
159-144

Middle Jurassic
190-159

Early Jurassic
205-190

Late Triassic
227-205

Middle Triassic
242-227

Early Triassic
245-242

Maiasaura

Pronounced *My-ah-saw-rah*

Maiasaura

Pronounced *My-ah-saw-rah*

When Horner and Makela discovered the large nesting site of Maiasaura it demonstrated for the first time the social, caring nature of some dinosaurs. The large number of nests showed that Maiasaura lived in herds, and possibly returned to the same site to nest every year, in a similar way that some birds do today. The nests were carefully arranged, about 7m (22ft 9in) apart, almost the size of an adult Maiasaura, and suggesting some form of caring. Each nest was about 2m (6ft 6in) in diameter and 0.75m (2ft 5in) deep, with a ring of heaped mud around it. Inside up to 20 eggs were carefully arranged in circles. At this important site there were also skeletons of hatchlings and baby Maiasaura in the nests, and young and adults nearby. There are signs that the babies had been fed by adult Maiasaura bringing vegetation to the nest. Such was the extent of the nest colony that the site where it was discovered became known as Egg Mountain. Maiasaura is a hadrosaur – a duck-billed dinosaur without a crest.

Meaning	Good Mother Lizard
When	Late Cretaceous
Time	84–71 million years ago
Max length	9m (29ft 3in)
Max height	3m (9ft 9in)
Max weight	4,500kg (9,900lb)
Stance	Quadruped/Biped
Where	USA (Montana)
Diet	Herbivore
Activity	Grazing
Intelligence	Medium
Named by	John Horner & Robert Makela
When named	1979
Order	Ornithischia (Bird-hipped)
Type	Ornithopoda, Hadrosauria

Late Cretaceous
99-65

Early Cretaceous
144-99

Late Jurassic
159-144

Middle Jurassic
190-159

Early Jurassic
205-190

Late Triassic
227-205

Middle Triassic
242-227

Early Triassic
245-242

Mamenchisaurus

Pronounced *Mah-men-che-saw-rus*

Mamenchisaurus

Pronounced *Mah-men-che-saw-rus*

Mamenchisaurus had the longest neck at 14m (45ft 6in) of any dinosaur, making up more than half of the dinosaur's total length. The neck was composed of 19 elongated vertebrae, which had long over-lapping bony struts that gave strength but hindered movement. The head was box-shaped with a blunt snout and spoon-shaped teeth for raking foliage off branches. Mamenchisaurus mainly fed off high coniferous trees. It was a slow mover and held its neck horizontal, parallel to the ground, when walking, but could raise it to feed. In common with other sauropods it had a lifespan of approximately 100 years, and reproduced by laying eggs. Despite the large size of sauropods, their eggs were no bigger than a grapefruit. Any larger and the shell would have had to be so thick that a baby dinosaur could not peck its way out. Fossilised sauropod eggs have been found in lines suggesting that they were laid whilst on the move, and that care was not taken of the babies. However sauropods lived in herds with adults and young together, partly as protection against predators.

Statistics

Meaning	Mamenchi Lizard
When	Late Jurassic
Time	154–151 million years ago
Max length	25m (81ft 3in)
Max height	11m (35ft 9in)
Max weight	20,000 (44,000lb)
Stance	Quadruped
Where	China
Diet	Herbivore
Activity	Grazing
Intelligence	Low
Named by	Chung Chien Young
When named	1954
Order	Saurischia (Lizard-hipped)
Type	Sauropodomorpha, Sauropoda

Timeline
Million Years Ago

Late Cretaceous
99–65

Early Cretaceous
144–99

Late Jurassic
159–144

Middle Jurassic
190–159

Early Jurassic
205–190

Late Triassic
227–205

Middle Triassic
242–227

Early Triassic
245–242

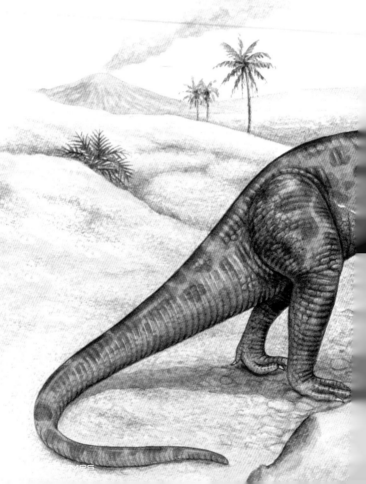

Massospondylus

Pronounced *Mass-oh-spon-dye-luss*

Massospondylus

Pronounced *Mass-oh-spon-dye-luss*

Massospondylus was extremely common in what is now southern Africa, as over 80 separate remains have been discovered. It has also been discovered in Arizona, USA, showing a wide distribution. This was possible because the continents were joined at the time in one enormous land-mass known as Pangaea. It was a medium sized prosauropod with a long neck and tail. The head was small with a variety of teeth in the jaws. This had lead to suggestions that it was a meat-eater, but it is now generally accepted that it was a plant-eater. This is supported by the discovery of gastroliths, or stomach stones, with its fossil bones. It walked on four legs but would rear up on its hind legs and feed off low trees. The hands were large with five fingers including a large thumb claw, which could have been used in defence or in mating contests. The prosauropods were a group of plant eating dinosaurs living in the Late Triassic and Early Jurassic times, and were the forerunners of the much larger sauropods.

Meaning	Massive Vertebra
When	Early Jurassic
Time	205–190 million years ago
Max length	4m (13ft)
Max height	1m (3ft 3in) at hips
Max weight	130kg (286lb)
Stance	Mainly Quadruped
Where	South Africa, Namibia, Lesotho, USA (Arizona)
Diet	Herbivore
Activity	Grazing
Intelligence	Low
Named by	Richard Owen
When named	1854
Order	Saurischia (Lizard-hipped)
Type	Sauropodomorpha, Prosauropoda

Late Cretaceous
99-65

Early Cretaceous
144-99

Late Jurassic
159-144

Middle Jurassic
190-159

Early Jurassic
205-190

Late Triassic
227-205

Middle Triassic
242-227

Early Triassic
245-242

Megalosaurus

Pronounced *Meg-ah-low-saw-rus*

Megalosaurus

Pronounced *Meg-ah-low-saw-rus*

This big, heavy-bodied dinosaur moved on two powerful legs. It was a typical carnosaur with three main toes with sharp claws (plus the trace of a fourth toe) on each foot. At the end of each short, strong arm was a three-clawed hand. The head was large, nearly one metre in length, and supported by a strong 'S' shaped neck. The long jaws held curved, saw-edged teeth flattened from side to side. The long tail balanced the weight of the body as it moved. One unique trackway of Megalosaurus, discovered in Dorset, England, and on display in The Dinosaur Museum, shows a 'tail-drag' impression. This proves that on occasions at least Megalosaurus walked with its tail on the ground. It was an excellent hunter attacking large plant-eating dinosaurs including some sauropods. Megalosaurus is an important dinosaur because it was the first one to be scientifically described and named. This first description was based on a jawbone. The very first remains, a thighbone, had been discovered by Robert Plot in 1676 and wrongly identified as belonging to a giant human being! Richard Owen later recognised this as another example of Megalosaurus.

Meaning	Great Lizard
When	Middle Jurassic
Time	180–169 million years ago
Max length	9m (30ft)
Max height	3m (9ft 9in)
Max weight	1,000kg (2,200lb)
Stance	Biped
Where	England & France
Diet	Carnivore
Activity	Hunting and possibly scavenging
Intelligence	Medium
Named by	Rev. William Buckland
When named	1824
Order	Saurischia (Lizard-hipped)
Type	Theropoda, Tetanurae, Carnosauria

Late Cretaceous
99-65

Early Cretaceous
144-99

Late Jurassic
159-144

Middle Jurassic
190-159

Early Jurassic
205-190

Late Triassic
227-205

Middle Triassic
242-227

Early Triassic
245-242

Muttaburrasaurus

Pronounced *Mut-ah-bur-ah-saw-rus*

Muttaburrasaurus

Pronounced *Mut-ah-bur-ah-saw-rus*

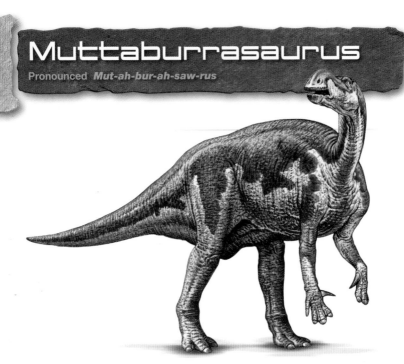

Muttaburrasaurus was the Australian equivalent of Iguanodon but smaller. The first remains were found in 1963 on Muttaburra Station, in Queensland, hence the dinosaur's name. By the early Cretaceous, Australia was a separate continent and Muttaburrasaurus remains have not been found anywhere else. It mainly lived on four legs but would have been able to rear up on its hind legs to feed from trees. It had a toothless beak like Iguanodon, but the cheek teeth were designed for shearing or slicing through food. This has led some palaeontologists to suggest that it sometimes ate meat, as well as grazing on cycads and conifers. There was a large bony bump on the snout, in front of the eyes, which may have contained nasal passages for amplifying calls, or may have been used for display purposes. The nostrils were unusually large suggesting that Muttaburrasaurus had a good sense of smell. Like Iguanodon the hands had five fingers including a thumb spike, and the hind legs were longer and more powerful than the front ones with three-toed feet.

Meaning	Muttaburra Station Lizard
When	Early Cretaceous
Time	112–99 million years ago
Max length	7m (22ft 9in)
Max height	4.5m (14ft 7in)
Max weight	4,100kg (9,000lb)
Stance	Quadruped
Where	Australia
Diet	Herbivore
Activity	Grazing
Intelligence	Medium
Named by	Alan Bartholomai & Ralph Molinar
When named	1981
Order	Ornithischia (Bird-hipped)
Type	Ornithopoda

Late Cretaceous
99-65

Early Cretaceous
144-99

Late Jurassic
159-144

Middle Jurassic
190-159

Early Jurassic
205-190

Late Triassic
227-205

Middle Triassic
242-227

Early Triassic
245-242

Ouranosaurus

Pronounced *Oo-rah-no-saw-rus*

Ouranosaurus

Pronounced *Oo-rah-no-saw-rus*

An almost complete skeleton of Ouranosaurus was discovered in 1966 in the Sahara Desert of Niger, in Africa. Its most distinctive feature is the row of spines that run down the back from the neck to almost the end of the tail. These spines are extensions of the individual bones in the backbone and a 'sail' of skin most likely covered them. This area of Africa was hot and dry in early Cretaceous times and a sail would have been useful as a temperature regulator. The sail would have been full of blood vessels that could either absorb or radiate heat as required. Spinosaurus, a 'sail-backed' meat-eating dinosaur also lived in the same area at the same time, suggesting that the 'sails' were a response to the climate. In most other aspects Ouranosaurus was very similar to Iguanodon. Ouranosaurus had a tough, horny, toothless beak with a large number of cheek teeth for grinding plants and vegetation. Its teeth and jaw muscles were weaker than those of Iguanodon.

Statistics

Meaning	Brave Lizard
When	Early Cretaceous
Time	121–112 million years ago
Max length	7m (22m 9in)
Max height	3m (9ft 9in)
Max weight	3,800kg (8,300lb)
Stance	Mainly Quadruped
Where	Niger
Diet	Herbivore
Activity	Grazing
Intelligence	Medium
Named by	Philippe Taquet
When named	1976
Order	Ornithischia (Bird-hipped)
Type	Ornithopoda

Timeline
Million Years Ago

Late Cretaceous
99-65

Early Cretaceous
144-99

Late Jurassic
159-144

Middle Jurassic
190-159

Early Jurassic
205-190

Late Triassic
227-205

Middle Triassic
242-227

Early Triassic
245-242

Oviraptor

Pronounced *Ov-ee-rap-tor*

Oviraptor

The first skeleton of Oviraptor was found in 1923 on top of a nest of what were thought to be Protoceratops eggs, and so it got its name as an 'egg thief'. In the 1990s further discoveries of eggs, nests and skeletons of Oviraptor actually on nests in an incubating position showed this was wrong, and that in fact it was protecting its nest. The eggs were about 13cm (5in) long and torpedo shaped. It was a bird-like dinosaur, covered in downy feathers for insulation. The head was small and the mouth and beak were completely toothless, except for two bony prongs to aid eating. It is uncertain what Oviraptor fed on, the jaws were strong and well muscled making it able to crush the bones of small animals, eggs or possibly even nuts. On top of the head was a hollow crest used for display purposes. Its legs and arms were long and slender with sharp claws on the end. It was a fast and agile runner and had large eyes for detecting prey.

Meaning	Egg Thief
When	Late Cretaceous
Time	84–71 million years ago
Max length	2.5m (8ft 1in)
Max height	0.9m (3ft)
Max weight	35kg (77lb)
Stance	Biped
Where	Mongolia
Diet	Omnivore
Activity	Hunting
Intelligence	High
Named by	Henry Osborn
When named	1924
Order	Saurischia (Lizard-hipped)
Type	Theropoda, Tetanurae, Coelurosauria

Timeline
Million Years Ago

Late Cretaceous
99-65

Early Cretaceous
144-99

Late Jurassic
159-144

Middle Jurassic
190-159

Early Jurassic
205-190

Late Triassic
227-205

Middle Triassic
242-227

Early Triassic
245-242

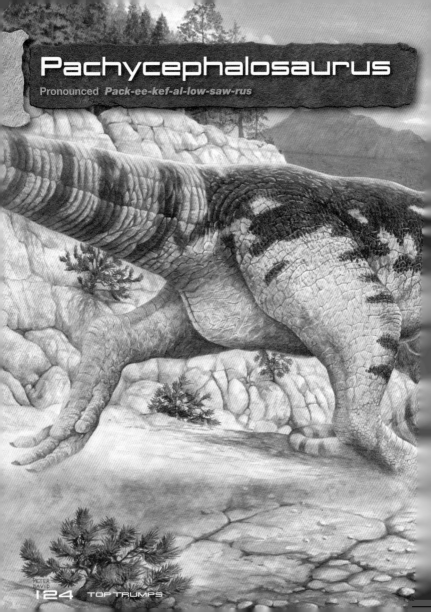

Pachycephalosaurus

Pronounced *Pack-ee-kef-al-low-saw-rus*

Pachycephalosaurus

Pronounced *Pack-ee-kef-al-low-saw-rus*

Pachycephalosaurus was one of the last dinosaurs living at the end of the Cretaceous period, just before the great extinction that wiped out all dinosaurs. It was the largest in the Pachycephalosaur 'bone head' family. The bony lump on its head, which gives it its name, was anything between 20 and 25cm (8–10in) thick. The traditional view is that it was used for head butting in defence or during fights for supremacy between two Pachycephalosaurus, just as stags do today. However two American scientists proposed a new theory in 2004 after detailed research. This was that Pachycephalosaurus would only have been able to head butt as a young dinosaur. As it became an adult the composition of the lump changed as it grew in size making it unsuitable for head butting. If this is true then the lump is more likely to be used for recognising different species and displaying. Bony nodules and spikes surrounded the bony lump and were probably to deter predators. Pachycephalosaurus had three types of teeth indicating a mixed diet from the abundant vegetation of the late Cretaceous.

Statistics

Meaning	Thick-headed Lizard
When	Late Cretaceous
Time	71–65 million years ago
Max length	5m (16ft 3in)
Max height	2.4m (7ft 9in)
Max weight	1,800kg (3,900lb)
Stance	Biped
Where	USA (Montana, Wyoming, Colorado, South Dakota)
Diet	Herbivore
Activity	Grazing
Intelligence	Medium
Named by	Barnum Brown & Erich Schlaiker
When named	1943
Order	Ornithischia (Bird-hipped)
Type	Marginocephalia, Pachycephalosauria

Timeline
Million Years Ago

Late Cretaceous	99-65
Early Cretaceous	144-99
Late Jurassic	159-144
Middle Jurassic	190-159
Early Jurassic	205-190
Late Triassic	227-205
Middle Triassic	242-227
Early Triassic	245-242

Panoplosaurus

Pronounced *Pan-oh-ploh-saw-rus*

The first fossil remains of Panoplosaurus were found in the Judith River
Formation in Alberta, Canada. Panoplosaurus was the last of the nodosaur
group of armoured dinosaurs. These were similar to ankylosaurs but did not
have a tail-club. This dinosaur was heavily armoured with thick bony square
plates, each with a central ridge, covering the back and embedded in the
skin. Both sides were protected by a row of short spikes running from the
neck to the end of the tail. The plates covering the head were actually fused to
the skull giving excellent protection. The skull was wide with a narrow snout
with which it foraged along the ground for suitable plants to eat. The front of
the mouth was toothless but the cheeks held leaf-shaped teeth for chewing
leaves. At the end of the Cretaceous period the vegetation was more diverse
than before and flowering plants had evolved for the first time. For its massive
size Panoplosaurus might have been fairly agile and would have charged at
any attacking carnivorous dinosaur to protect itself.

Statistics

Meaning	Fully Armoured Lizard
When	Late Cretaceous
Time	84–71 million years ago
Max length	7m (22ft 9in)
Max height	2.3m (7ft 6in)
Max weight	3,000kg (6,613lb)
Stance	Quadruped
Where	USA (Montana, South Dakota, Texas), Canada (Alberta)
Diet	Herbivore
Activity	Grazing
Intelligence	Low
Named by	Lawrence Lambe
When named	1919
Order	Ornithischia (Bird-hipped)
Type	Thyreophora, Ankylosauria

Timeline
Million Years Ago

Late Cretaceous
99-65

Early Cretaceous
144-99

Late Jurassic
159-144

Middle Jurassic
190-159

Early Jurassic
205-190

Late Triassic
227-205

Middle Triassic
242-227

Early Triassic
245-242

Parasaurolophus

Pronounced *Para-saw-row-low-fuss*

Parasaurolophus

Parasaurolophus was the most spectacular of the duck-billed dinosaurs with a long backward-curving crest attached to its head. The crest was up to 1.8m (5ft 10in) long with hollow nasal passages running the complete length and back again. It is thought that these nasal passages were used to amplify calls, creating a trumpet effect. Parasaurolophus had no means of defence so perhaps they called warnings to each other of potential attacks. As all the Lambeosaurine dinosaurs had different shaped crests it is most probable that the shape of the crest determined the type of call. Males had longer crests than females meaning that the different sexes would have had different calls as well. There may have been a flap of skin between the crest and the back of the neck, which Parasaurolophus used for display. The backbone had a notch at the point where the end of the crest touched it, which was most likely for the crest to rest on. It walked mainly on all four legs, however the hind legs were strong enough for it to rear up to feed off trees.

Meaning	Beside Crested Lizard
When	Late Cretaceous
Time	84–65 million years ago
Max length	10m (32ft 6in)
Max height	4.9m (12ft)
Max weight	5,000 (11,000lb)
Stance	Mainly Quadruped
Where	Canada (Alberta), USA (New Mexico, Utah)
Diet	Herbivore
Activity	Grazing
Intelligence	Medium
Named by	William Parks
When named	1922
Order	Ornithischia (Bird-hipped)
Type	Ornithopoda, Hadrosauria

Late Cretaceous
99-65

Early Cretaceous
144-99

Late Jurassic
159-144

Middle Jurassic
190-159

Early Jurassic
205-190

Late Triassic
227-205

Middle Triassic
242-227

Early Triassic
245-242

Plateosaurus

Pronounced *Plat-ee-oh-saw-rus*

Plateosaurus

Pronounced *Plat-ee-oh-saw-rus*

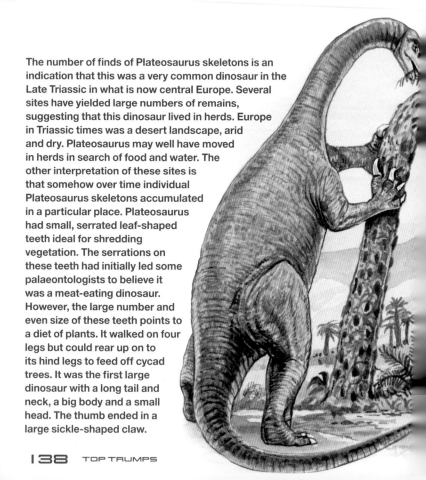

The number of finds of Plateosaurus skeletons is an indication that this was a very common dinosaur in the Late Triassic in what is now central Europe. Several sites have yielded large numbers of remains, suggesting that this dinosaur lived in herds. Europe in Triassic times was a desert landscape, arid and dry. Plateosaurus may well have moved in herds in search of food and water. The other interpretation of these sites is that somehow over time individual Plateosaurus skeletons accumulated in a particular place. Plateosaurus had small, serrated leaf-shaped teeth ideal for shredding vegetation. The serrations on these teeth had initially led some palaeontologists to believe it was a meat-eating dinosaur. However, the large number and even size of these teeth points to a diet of plants. It walked on four legs but could rear up on to its hind legs to feed off cycad trees. It was the first large dinosaur with a long tail and neck, a big body and a small head. The thumb ended in a large sickle-shaped claw.

Statistics

Meaning	Broad lizard
When	Late Triassic
Time	221–210 million years ago
Max length	8m (26ft)
Max height	1.5m (4ft 10in) at hips
Max weight	1,800kg (3,900lb)
Stance	Quadruped
Where	Germany, Switzerland & France
Diet	Herbivore
Activity	Grazing
Intelligence	Low
Named by	Hermann von Meyer
When named	1837
Order	Saurischia (Lizard-hipped)
Type	Sauropodomorpha, Prosauropoda

Timeline
Million Years Ago

Late Cretaceous
99–65

Early Cretaceous
144–99

Late Jurassic
159–144

Middle Jurassic
190–159

Early Jurassic
205–190

Late Triassic
227–205

Middle Triassic
242–227

Early Triassic
245–242

Protoceratops

Pronounced *Pro-toe-sair-ah-tops*

Many hundreds of skeletons of Protoceratops have been found, particularly by the expeditions of the American Museum of Natural History to Mongolia, between 1922 and 1925. Numerous eggs and over 100 skeletons were discovered at the Flaming Cliffs, named after the bright red sand, in southern Mongolia. The eggs are torpedo shaped, about 20cm (8in) long, and were arranged in a spiral pattern in nests. A famous fossil was discovered in 1971 of the skeletons of Protoceratops and Velociraptor locked in battle. Both fought to the death and were possibly overcome by some natural disaster. Protoceratops could inflict some damage to an attacker with its strong beak. It was a common dinosaur during the Late Cretaceous living in large herds. It had a bony frill to protect the head and neck, but unlike other ceratopsian dinosaurs it did not have any horns. There was a difference between the sexes with males being more powerful, with a larger frill and a larger bump on the end of the snout. This may have been used for head-butting contests.

Meaning	First Horned Face
When	Late Cretaceous
Time	86–71 million years ago
Max length	2.5m (8ft 2in)
Max height	0.9m (2ft 11in)
Max weight	400kg (880lb)
Stance	Quadruped
Where	Mongolia & China
Diet	Herbivore
Activity	Grazing
Intelligence	Low
Named by	Walter Granger & William Gregory
When named	1923
Order	Ornithischia (Bird-hipped)
Type	Marginocephalia, Ceratopsia

Late Cretaceous
99-65

Early Cretaceous
144-99

Late Jurassic
159-144

Middle Jurassic
190-159

Early Jurassic
205-190

Late Triassic
227-205

Middle Triassic
242-227

Early Triassic
245-242

Psittacosaurus

Psittacosaurus

Pronounced *Sit-ah-co-saw-rus*

Psittacosaurus gets its name from the shape of the toothless curved beak and the rather strange shape of the head. It was an early form of ceratopsian dinosaur and the cheeks had already started to form a small bony horn on each side. It had not yet developed the bony frill or horns that distinguished ceratopsians from other dinosaurs. Ceratopsians were quadrupeds yet Psittacosaurus mainly walked on two long powerful rear legs, and only occasionally moving on all four limbs. The arms were shorter with four fingered hands for gathering food. Behind the beak were rows of sharp teeth for chopping up plants for digestion in the stomach. This was aided by gastroliths (stomach stones) which have been found with some skeletons. Its only means of defence from predators was to run. Two Psittacosaurus specimens were first discovered in Mongolia in 1922 and they caused much confusion. Initially it was thought that they were two different dinosaurs and that they were closely related to Hypsilophodon. In 1923 two very young Psittacosaurus were discovered.

Meaning	Parrot Lizard
When	Early Cretaceous
Time	121–112 million years ago
Max length	2m (6ft 5in)
Max height	1m (3ft 3in)
Max weight	80kg (176lb)
Stance	Biped
Where	Mongolia, China & Thailand
Diet	Herbivore
Activity	Grazing
Intelligence	Low
Named by	Henry Fairfield Osborn
When named	1923
Order	Ornithischia (Bird-hipped)
Type	Marginocephalia, Ceratopsia

Late Cretaceous
99–65

Early Cretaceous
144–99

Late Jurassic
159–144

Middle Jurassic
190–159

Early Jurassic
205–190

Late Triassic
227–205

Middle Triassic
242–227

Early Triassic
245–242

Scelidosaurus

Pronounced *Skel-id-oh-saw-rus*

Scelidosaurus

Pronounced *Skel-id-oh-saw-rus*

In Dorset, England, Scelidosaurus has been found only in marine deposits more commonly known for ichthyosaur and plesiosaur remains. The carcasses of Scelidosaurus were probably washed down a river into the sea to become fossilised. It is a fairly primitive dinosaur, originally thought to be an ancestor of the stegosaurs but now thought to be an early ankylosaur. The whole of the upper side of the body was covered by parallel rows of bony scutes and a row of short spines. The small horny beak has six teeth with leaf-shaped cheek teeth behind. The rear legs were longer and more powerful than the front, but it was still a quadrupedal dinosaur. The initial bones named by Richard Owen as Scelidosaurus were much later found to be a mixture of species. The identification was then given to the later 1863 skeleton. It was Richard Owen who in 1841 had invented the word 'dinosauria', meaning 'terrible lizard', to describe the group of extinct reptiles that were beginning to be discovered, of which Megalosaurus and Iguanodon were members.

Meaning	Rear Leg Lizard
When	Early Jurassic
Time	202–190 million years ago
Max length	4m (13ft)
Max height	1.1m (3ft 6in)
Max weight	350kg (770lb)
Stance	Quadruped
Where	England & USA (Arizona)
Diet	Herbivore
Activity	Grazing
Intelligence	Low
Named by	Richard Owen
When named	1863
Order	Ornithischia (Bird-hipped)
Type	Thyreophora, Ankylosauria

Timeline
Million Years Ago

Late Cretaceous
99-65

Early Cretaceous
144-99

Late Jurassic
159-144

Middle Jurassic
190-159

Early Jurassic
205-190

Late Triassic
227-205

Middle Triassic
242-227

Early Triassic
245-242

Seismosaurus

Pronounced *Size-mow-saw-rus*

Only one skeleton of Seismosaurus has ever been found, and that was in 1979 by two walkers in the fossil-rich Morrison Formation of New Mexico. They discovered some of the tail-bones and proper excavations followed in 1985. Ground-penetrating radar was used to aid palaeontologists in establishing the full extent of the skeleton. It was a massive sauropod, certainly the longest known dinosaur at up to 40m from the small head to the tip of the tail. Along with Supersaurus, Argentinosaurus and Amphicoelias, it was one of the biggest dinosaurs ever. About 250 gastroliths (stomach stones) were found with the skeleton, confirming that at least some sauropods used them to aid digestion. The teeth were peg-like and only suitable for stripping leaves off branches. The gastroliths, which averaged about 5cm (2in) across, were held in a muscular gizzard and helped to grind down and break up tough vegetation, before it was passed further though the digestive system. Like Diplodocus, Seismosaurus was lightly built for its size, and the long neck and tail were strengthened by bony projections.

Meaning	Earthquake Lizard
When	Late Jurassic
Time	154–151 million years ago
Max length	40m (130ft)
Max height	5.5m (17ft 10in) at hips
Max weight	30,000kg (66,100lb)
Stance	Quadruped
Where	USA (New Mexico)
Diet	Herbivore
Activity	Grazing
Intelligence	Low
Named by	David Gillette
When named	1991
Order	Saurischia (Lizard-hipped)
Type	Sauropodomorpha, Sauropoda

Late Cretaceous
99-65

Early Cretaceous
144-99

Late Jurassic
159-144

Middle Jurassic
190-159

Early Jurassic
205-190

Late Triassic
227-205

Middle Triassic
242-227

Early Triassic
245-242

Sinosauropteryx

Pronounced *Sigh-no-saw-op-ter-ix*

Sinosauropteryx

Pronounced *Sigh-no-saw-op-ter-ix*

The discovery of Sinosauropteryx in 1996 caused tremendous excitement and changed the whole understanding of dinosaurs. Until then all dinosaurs were believed to have reptilian scaly skin and some skin impressions had been found that confirmed this theory. Sinosauropteryx was discovered in the fine-grained rocks of the Yixian Formation in the Liaoning Province of China. These rocks were similar to those of Solonhofen in Germany, where Archaeopteryx was found, and were ideal for preserving detailed fossil remains. Sinosauropteryx was covered with short, simple feathers known as protofeathers, about 3.5cm (1.5in) long. These protofeathers were comprised of single filaments and would have formed a downy covering over the dinosaur giving excellent insulation. They were not suitable for flying, but their presence suggests that it was a warm-blooded animal. Apart from the feathers Sinosauropteryx was much like any small, long-legged coelurosaur. It would have hunted small animals of the time; indeed one skeleton had a small mammal preserved in its stomach. Other feathered dinosaurs from the Liaoning Province are Dilong, Caudipteryx and Microraptor, which show varying degrees of feather development.

Meaning	Chinese Lizard Feathered
When	Early Cretaceous
Time	127–121 million years ago
Max length	0.5m (1ft 8in)
Max height	0.3m (1ft)
Max weight	3kg (7lb)
Stance	Biped
Where	China
Diet	Carnivore
Activity	Hunting
Intelligence	High
Named by	Ji Qiang
When named	1996
Order	Saurischia (Lizard-hipped)
Type	Theropoda, Tetanurae, Coelurosauria

Late Cretaceous
99-65

Early Cretaceous
144-99

Late Jurassic
159-144

Middle Jurassic
190-159

Early Jurassic
205-190

Late Triassic
227-205

Middle Triassic
242-227

Early Triassic
245-242

Spinosaurus

Pronounced *Spy-no-saw-rus*

Spinosaurus

Pronounced *Spy-no-saw-rus*

The first and best example of Spinosaurus was discovered and named by Ernst Stromer in 1912 in Egypt. Unfortunately the skeleton became another casualty of Allied bombing during World War 2. Further partial discoveries were made in 1996. Studies of these discoveries, particularly of the snout, suggest that Spinosaurus was the largest meat-eating dinosaur, longer even than either Giganotosaurus or Tyrannosaurus rex. It had a long snout of 99cm (3ft 2in), similar to that of a crocodile. Spinosaurus takes its name from its most distinctive feature: a row of bony spines, over 1.5m (5ft) long, attached to the backbone. These were covered with skin to form a 'sail', which was most likely used as a heat exchanger to either absorb or radiate heat. Another purpose may have been to signal or display. The teeth were long, straight and conical, and this combined with the long snout and the discovery of a fish bone among the teeth suggests that Spinosaurus fed mainly off fish. However, it would have probably scavenged or hunted dinosaurs to obtain additional food.

Statistics

Meaning	Spiny Lizard
When	Cretaceous
Time	112–94 million years ago
Max length	17m (55ft 3in)
Max height	6.75m (22ft)
Max weight	9,000kg (19,800lb)
Stance	Biped
Where	Egypt & Morocco
Diet	Carnivore
Activity	Hunting
Intelligence	Medium
Named by	Ernst Stromer
When named	1915
Order	Saurischia (Lizard-hipped)
Type	Theropoda, Tetanurae, Carnosauria

Timeline
Million Years Ago

Late Cretaceous
99–65

Early Cretaceous
144–99

Late Jurassic
159–144

Middle Jurassic
190–159

Early Jurassic
205–190

Late Triassic
227–205

Middle Triassic
242–227

Early Triassic
245–242

Stegosaurus

Pronounced *Steg-oh-saw-rus*

Stegosaurus

Pronounced *Steg-oh-saw-rus*

This armoured dinosaur was distinguished by two rows of alternating bony plates, over 60cm (2ft) high, along the back and tail. The plates contained blood vessels and most likely acted as temperature regulators, either dispersing or absorbing heat. This indicates that Stegosaurus was a cold-blooded dinosaur, getting its energy from the sun rather than from food. The plates may also have been used for defence. However Stegosaurus had spikes, up to 1m (3ft 3in) long, on the end of its flexible tail with which to defend itself. There were either four or eight spikes depending on the species. Bony scutes or studs protected parts of the body. The small head was held very close to the ground, as the front legs were much shorter than the rear ones. Its beak was toothless, but there were some weak cheek teeth further back. Stegosaurus fed off low vegetation such as ferns and horsetails. Stegosaurus is famous for its tiny brain, only the size of a walnut, making it one of the least intelligent dinosaurs.

Meaning	Roofed Lizard
When	Late Jurassic
Time	156–144 million years ago
Max length	9m (30ft)
Max height	2.75m (9ft) at hips
Max weight	2,700kg (5,900lb)
Stance	Quadruped
Where	USA (Wyoming, Colorado, Utah & Oklahoma)
Diet	Herbivore
Activity	Browsing possibly in herds
Intelligence	Low
Named by	Othniel Charles Marsh
When named	1877
Order	Ornithischia (Bird-hipped)
Type	Thyreophora, Stegosauria

Late Cretaceous 99-65

Early Cretaceous 144-99

Late Jurassic 159-144

Middle Jurassic 190-159

Early Jurassic 205-190

Late Triassic 227-205

Middle Triassic 242-227

Early Triassic 245-242

Therizinosaurus

Pronounced *Ther-eye-zin-oh-saw-rus*

Therizinosaurus

Pronounced *Ther-eye-zin-oh-saw-rus*

Therizinosaurus was a strange-looking dinosaur of which little is actually known, as only fragmentary remains have been found so far. It was first discovered in 1948 and has proved a puzzle since then. When discovered it was thought that it was a 'turtle-like lizard'. It takes its name from the three long curving claws, the longest of which was 70cm (2ft 3in), on each hand. The purpose of these has been much disputed. They seem too blunt for attacking prey, ruling out a meat diet. Other suggestions have been that they were used for catching fish, or opening termite mounds. The most likely use is for gathering branches and fronds of plants. It has been suggested that Therizinosaurus might have squatted down and fed in a similar way to a gorilla. Therizinosaurus had a weak neck, a small head and a toothless beak. It was an extremely unusual theropod with small, leaf-shaped teeth pointing to an herbivorous diet.

Meaning	Scythe Lizard
When	Late Cretaceous
Time	84–71 million years ago
Max length	11m (35ft 9in)
Max height	4m (13ft)
Max weight	3,000kg (6,600lb)
Stance	Biped
Where	Mongolia
Diet	Probably Herbivore
Activity	Probably grazing
Intelligence	Medium
Named by	Evgenii Maleev
When named	1954
Order	Saurischia (Lizard-hipped)
Type	Theropoda, Tetanurae, Segnosauria

Late Cretaceous
99-65

Early Cretaceous
144-99

Late Jurassic
159-144

Middle Jurassic
190-159

Early Jurassic
205-190

Late Triassic
227-205

Middle Triassic
242-227

Early Triassic
245-242

Triceratops

Pronounced *Try-seer-ah-tops*

Triceratops

Pronounced *Try-seer-ah-tops*

Triceratops is named after the three horns that protrude from the large bony frill that covered the head and protected the neck. The front horn on the snout was short, whilst the horns over each eye were about 1m (3ft 3in) long. Triceratops would have probably charged any predator using a combination of its weight and its horns and frill to fight off any potential attack. One of these predators was Tyrannosaurus rex. Around the edge of the frill were small bony spikes for added protection. The skull was enormous, forming almost one-third of the entire length of the dinosaur. Many skulls and horns show scars from damage caused by combat. Triceratops may have locked horns in fights for supremacy with other Triceratops. It was a common dinosaur, living right at the end of the dinosaur era, and many remains have been found. It lived in herds feeding off low-growing plants such as cycads and ferns, which it would have nipped off with its horny beak and then chewed up with its cheek teeth.

Statistics

Meaning	Three Horned Face
When	Late Cretaceous
Time	71–65 million years ago
Max length	9m (30ft)
Max height	3m (10ft) at hips
Max weight	10,000kg (22,046lb)
Stance	Quadruped
Where	USA (Colorado, Montana, Wyoming, South Dakota,) Canada (Alberta, Saskatchewan)
Diet	Herbivore
Activity	Grazing in herds
Intelligence	Medium
Named by	Othniel Charles Marsh
When named	1889
Order	Ornithischia (Bird-hipped)
Type	Marginocephalia, Ceratopsia

Timeline
Million Years Ago

Late Cretaceous	99–65
Early Cretaceous	144–99
Late Jurassic	159–144
Middle Jurassic	190–159
Early Jurassic	205–190
Late Triassic	227–205
Middle Triassic	242–227
Early Triassic	245–242

Troodon

Pronounced *Trew-oh-don*

Troodon

Pronounced *Trew-oh-don*

Troodon had a very large brain compared to its body size, suggesting that it was highly intelligent. The long head held two large eyes, which gave excellent vision and indicate that it was a night hunter. If this was the case then Troodon was a warm-blooded dinosaur. It would not have had the energy to hunt after dark if it was cold-blooded. It fed off small mammals, reptiles and dinosaurs. Troodon had one large sickle-shaped claw on the second toe of each foot, similar to Deinonychus, but not as large. The hands had three long claws for grasping and holding prey, and the long stiff tail would have balanced the dinosaur whilst running fast. Troodon is named after the original tooth found in 1854. Initially Troodon was portrayed with a reptilian skin texture, but more recent evidence has led to new interpretations as a feathered dinosaur. The downy feathers were not for flight but to insulate the dinosaur, which would have been especially important if it was warm-blooded.

Statistics

Meaning	Wounding Tooth
When	Late Cretaceous
Time	76–65 million years ago
Max length	2m (6ft 6in)
Max height	1m (3ft 3in)
Max weight	50kg (110lb)
Stance	Biped
Where	Canada (Alberta), USA (Montana, Wyoming)
Diet	Carnivore
Activity	Agile hunter
Intelligence	Very High
Named by	Joseph Leidy
When named	1856
Order	Saurischia (Lizard-hipped)
Type	Theropoda, Tetanurae, Coelurosauria

Timeline
Million Years Ago

Late Cretaceous
99-65

Early Cretaceous
144-99

Late Jurassic
159-144

Middle Jurassic
190-159

Early Jurassic
205-190

Late Triassic
227-205

Middle Triassic
242-227

Early Triassic
245-242

Tyrannosaurus rex

Pronounced *Tie-ran-oh-saw-rus rex*

Tyrannosaurus rex

Pronounced *Tie-ran-oh-saw-rus rex*

Tyrannosaurus rex is the most famous of all the dinosaurs. For a long time it held the record as the largest meat-eating dinosaur ever, until Giganotosaurus was discovered. The skull of T rex was large with strong jaws containing curved, serrated teeth up to 15cm (6in) long. It had powerful legs but ridiculously short arms with two-clawed hands the purpose of which is not known. There has been much debate as to whether T rex was a hunter or a scavenger. One argument is that if it fell whilst chasing prey it would not have been able to raise itself again, and therefore it must have scavenged. The other argument is that it had stereoscopic eyesight and could therefore judge distances, a good sense of smell and, although not particularly fast, could still ambush and kill prey. The truth is probably that T rex was both hunter and scavenger. Fossilised dung, known as coprolites, show that the main diet was plant-eating dinosaurs such as Triceratops and duck-billed dinosaurs. Tyrannosaurids are classified as coelurosaurs and not carnosaurs as might be expected from their size.

Statistics

Meaning	Tyrant Lizard King
When	Late Cretaceous
Time	71–65 million years ago
Max length	12.8m (41ft 6in)
Max height	5.5m (17ft 9in)
Max weight	7,000kg (14,100lb)
Stance	Biped
Where	USA (Colorado, Montana, Wyoming, Texas) Canada (Alberta, Saskatchewan)
Diet	Carnivore
Activity	Hunting and/or scavenging
Intelligence	Medium
Named by	Henry Fairfield Osborn
When named	1905
Order	Saurischia (Lizard-hipped)
Type	Theropoda, Tetanurae, Coelurosauria

Timeline
Million Years Ago

Late Cretaceous
99–65

Early Cretaceous
144–99

Late Jurassic
159–144

Middle Jurassic
190–159

Early Jurassic
205–190

Late Triassic
227–205

Middle Triassic
242–227

Early Triassic
245–242

Velociraptor

Pronounced *Vel-oh-see-rap-tor*

Velociraptor

Pronounced *Vel-oh-see-rap-tor*

Velociraptor was another discovery first made by a team from the American Museum of Natural History in 1923 at Mongolia's Flaming Cliffs. It was a swift and fierce predator with three-clawed grasping hands, and the second toe of each foot held a large sickle shaped claw. In 1971 a spectacular fossil discovery was made of the skeletons of Velociraptor and Protoceratops locked in combat. Velocirator's hands were grasping the head of Protoceratops and the sickle claw was buried in its stomach. Protoceratops had defended itself and inflicted some injuries on Velociraptor, probably with its beak. It is thought both were overcome by a sandstorm. Velociraptors also fought amongst themselves. A fossil skull shows teeth marks from another Velociraptor proving that it was killed by one of its own kind. Velociraptor was a fast and agile runner and used its long straight tail to balance when moving. The snout was long and flattened, setting it apart from other dromaeosaurids. Like most other coelurosaurs it was at least partially covered in downy feathers.

Statistics

Meaning	Speedy Thief
When	Late Cretaceous
Time	84–71 million years ago
Max length	1.8m (5ft 10in)
Max height	0.9m (2ft 11in)
Max weight	30kg (66lb)
Stance	Biped
Where	Mongolia & China
Diet	Carnivore
Activity	Hunting
Intelligence	High
Named by	Henry Fairfield Osborn
When named	1924
Order	Saurischia (Lizard-hipped)
Type	Theropoda, Tetanurae, Coelurosauria

Timeline
Million Years Ago

Late Cretaceous
99–65

Early Cretaceous
144–99

Late Jurassic
159–144

Middle Jurassic
190–159

Early Jurassic
205–190

Late Triassic
227–205

Middle Triassic
242–227

Early Triassic
245–242

Checklist

 Allosaurus
Date   Location

 Amargasaurus
Date   Location

 Ankylosaurus
Date   Location

 Archaeopteryx
Date   Location

 Baryonyx
Date   Location

 Brachiosaurus
Date   Location

 Camarasaurus
Date   Location

 Carcharodontosaurus
Date   Location

 Carnotaurus
Date   Location

 Ceratosaurus
Date   Location

Coelophysis
Date   Location

Compsognathus
Date   Location

Dilophosaurus
Date   Location

Diplodocus
Date   Location

Eoraptor
Date   Location

Gallimimus
Date   Location

Giganotosaurus
Date   Location

Herrerasaurus
Date   Location

Hypsilophodon
Date   Location

Iguanodon
Date   Location

Kentrosaurus
Date   Location

		Lambeosaurus Date · Location
		Maiasaura Date · Location
		Mamenchisaurus Date · Location
		Massospondylus Date · Location
		Megalosaurus Date · Location
		Muttaburrasaurus Date · Location
		Ouranosaurus Date · Location
		Oviraptor Date · Location
		Pachycephalosaurus Date · Location
		Panoplosaurus Date · Location
		Parasaurolophus Date · Location
		Plateosaurus Date · Location